RAILWAY A
IN PICT

TRA
in
TROUBLE

ALAN EARNSHAW

CW01665288

VOLUME SEVEN

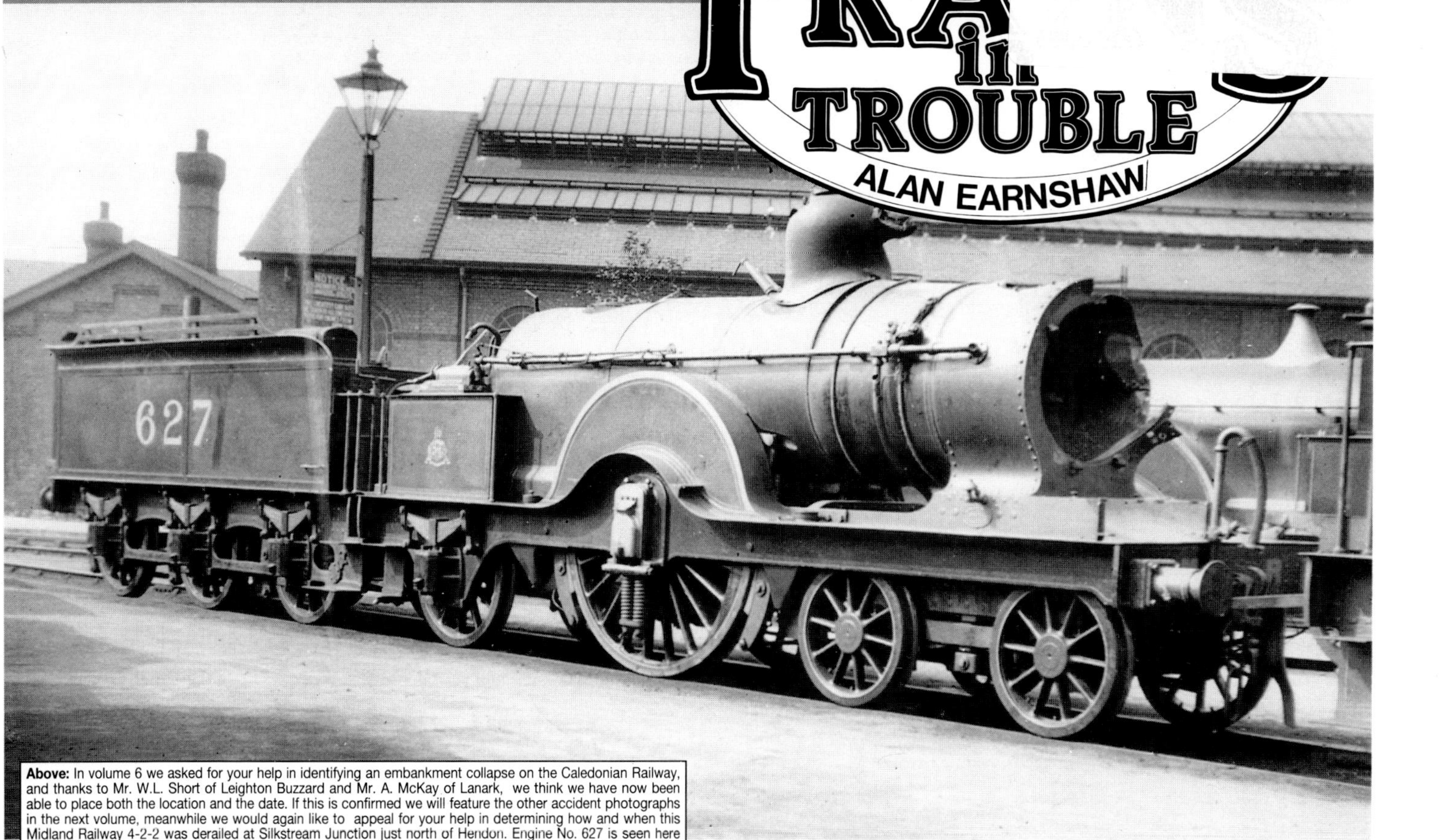

Above: In volume 6 we asked for your help in identifying an embankment collapse on the Caledonian Railway, and thanks to Mr. W.L. Short of Leighton Buzzard and Mr. A. McKay of Lanark, we think we have now been able to place both the location and the date. If this is confirmed we will feature the other accident photographs in the next volume, meanwhile we would again like to appeal for your help in determining how and when this Midland Railway 4-2-2 was derailed at Silkstream Junction just north of Hendon. Engine No. 627 is seen here at Kentish Town, but if you can help with information, we will also feature the actual accident pictures in the next Trains In Trouble.

Front Cover: Our three jacket illustrations are all from the modern-era, and represent potentially major disasters which all had relatively minor consequences. Our cover picture was taken on 3 May 1979, after a north-bound train from St. Blazey had been derailed at Settle Junction. As a consequence china-clay wagons piled up behind the locomotive and the line was completely blocked. fortunately the accident happened just moments after a Leeds-bound train had passed on the Up Line, and thereby narrowly missed causing a double derailment. *Colour Slide by P. Robinson.*

Rear Cover, Upper: The picture of these buckled vehicles at Bradford on Tone (Somerset), intimates the ferocity of a massive fireball which consumed a train of derailed oil tankers on 16 May 1991. The train was the 4.10 am from Milford Haven to Heathfield, comprised of 22 private owner oil tankers carrying kerosene, diesel and petrol. Sixteen of the 22 and 45-tonne vehicles caught fire and eight of these exploded, resulting in a blaze which took 15 fire crews seven hours to control. The accident could have had serious consequences coupled with major ecological problems but as, will be detailed in Volume 8, things were nowhere near as bad as they could have been. *Sarah Earnshaw.*

Rear Cover, Lower: This dramatic night-time view on 23 November 1983, reveals yet another narrow escape was experienced by passengers on the 21.35 pm night sleeper from Penzance. As No. 50041 *Bulwark*, approached Paddington, it suffered a high-speed derailment on a 25 mph crossover at 6.11 during the final minutes of the journey. fortunately, no-one was badly injured, as the strength of modern coaching stock prevented a major disaster. *Colour Slide by Hugh Daddy.*

Designed by Barnabus Design, Truro, Cornwall.
Typeset by TypeStyle, Truro, Cornwall.
Printed by Century Litho, Penryn, Cornwall.
Bound by Booth Bookbinders, Penryn, Cornwall.

First Published 1991. ISBN 0 906899 50 8

No part of this publication may be reproduced in any form or by any means without prior written permission of the publishers.

© Atlantic Transport Publishers and Alan Earnshaw, 1991.

PUBLISHED BY

Atlantic

ATLANTIC TRANSPORT PUBLISHERS
TREVITHICK HOUSE · WEST END
PENRYN · CORNWALL TR10 8HE

CONTENTS

INTRODUCTION

When Trains In Trouble was first released, it was only ever intended that the series would run to four volumes. However as original stocks became depleted, popular demand led to a re-print of the first four books in 1989, accompanied by two new volumes released in 1989-90. This was intended as the climax of the series, leaving any other major accidents to be covered in Atlantic's bi-monthly magazine BACKTRACK. Yet, even as I wrote the final words of Volume 6, late in November 1989, I had a feeling that perhaps we had not quite seen the end of Trains In Trouble as many of our readers asked us to extend the series by covering a number of specific accidents. Since then a veritable flood of photographic material covering several notable and historic accidents has found its way to my home, along with more than one or two observations that I had erroneously placed Wynmondham Junction in Norfolk when in fact it was in Leicestershire - thanks to all concerned and my apologies to Mr. Clay for not listening in my geography lessons all those years ago!

As the 'new' material we had been sent accounted for a substantial number of the 'unknown' accident photographs, we decided to produce this volume, and possibly one more. After the last time, I would not categorically state that these are the last books, but it seems as though we are now nearing the end, having covered every conceivable aspect of railway disaster, and included the majority of notable accidents. As it is not our intention to consistently keep offering 'warmed-up left-overs', we have made a conscious effort to discuss the major accidents left un-covered from earlier volumes.

Naturally the books do not cover all the incidents and accidents recorded, and even some fatal accidents have been deliberately ignored. To help the reader understand why certain accidents were chosen whilst others have been omitted, it is perhaps prudent to explain our criteria for choosing the material for inclusion. Firstly we set a time period, 1870 - 1970, this being because 1870 is really the earliest we can expect to find comprehensive photographic coverage of an accident (particularly press coverage); whilst we set a decency rule, not allowing serious accidents within the past 20 years to be covered. This latter aspect may be disappointing to those who particularly want to see pictures of diesel and electric locomotives in trouble, but recounting events of more recent times can still be very painful to the families of those involved. Whilst I do not pander to a 'steam only' concept, it can not be ignored that a very high percentage of the total number of accidents reported since 1840 involved steam locomotives and the pictures chosen reflect this.

Two other factors presented themselves as important criteria in the selection of which accidents still required coverage. Firstly, it was our intention not to look solely at the element of human error, as many readers have asked us to cover the technical and operational considerations behind the accidents we have selected. Secondly, in order to provide something new, we had to see wether the accident concerned had been covered in any other recent publication, and if so, if it was accompanied by photographs. For example, the classic 'Red For Danger' by L.T.C. Rolt discusses 97 accidents within our given period, only a few of which had accompanying illustrations. Over half of these accidents had not been pictorially covered in Trains in Trouble or contemporary publications.

After combing the accident report statistics and comparing this with our 'criteria', it left around 72 major accidents un-covered. Having set this as an achievable target the work on finding and sorting photographs began. However in order to include as many of this number as possible, the balance between serious and non-serious accidents has had to be amended. Previously I had aimed at an equal balance between fatal and non-serious accidents, but in the remaining books there are bound to be far more of the former. In view of this, I have generally omitted the names of the individuals named in the various accident reports. It has also been impossible to maintain a fair regional coverage, but such a concept was always hard to achieve given the magnificent safety record of the GWR.

Finally it is perhaps a fitting tribute to say that volume 7 has been prepared in 1990, which is the 150th anniversary of that august body, the Inspecting Officers of Railways. Since their authorisation by Act of Parliament in 1840, these men have carefully and meticulously investigated every serious accident, and many minor ones, with one aim in mind - the overall safety of the travelling public. So; though the following pages may be a testimony to error, mis-judgement, stupidity, and even flagrant breeches of regulations; we can be assured that such scenes would have been repeated many, many times over, had it not been for the various safety regulations devised and introduced largely on the insistence of these inspectors appointed by the Board of Trade and its successors.

Alan Earnshaw,
Houses Hill, W.Yorks. December 1990

A train in Trouble, ex-Midland Railway compound No.1010, which featured in two accidents at exactly the same place. Seen awaiting attention in Carlisle, August 1933, the full story is recounted on page 23.
Photograph courtesy: K. Longbottom Collection.

STAPLEHURST (SER)
9 June 1865

In Volume 6, we touched briefly on the experiences of novelist Charles Dickens in a railway accident at Staplehurst, though at the time we were unable to find any photographic record of the event. However, we now have to hand this view of the incident, in which ten of Dickens' co-travellers regretfully lost their lives when the 'Up Tidal' train was derailed over the Beult Viaduct.

For a period of ten weeks prior to the accident, the SER had been replacing the longtitudinal timbers on three low viaducts in the section from Ashford to Staplehurst. The normal policy had been to replace these baulks in the intervals when the line was quiet, as opposed to taking complete possession of one line and introducing 'single-line working'. Though this arrangement was questionable, it had worked well during that time, with the permanent way staff breaking the rails after the trains had passed, renewing the timber and then replacing the rail before the next one came. This was no great difficulty, as there were several sizeable intervals in the timetable which gave sufficient time to accomplish the tasks. Out of 32 baulks which had to be replaced, just one more was left to be done, and on 9 June the rail over the Beult Viaduct was broken after the 2.51pm Up train had passed by. The foreman platelayer believed that the next train was not due until 4.15pm, however he had mis-read the timetable and not made allowances for the 'Tidal' express. This working, as its name implies, was timed to leave Folkestone in connection with tidal shipping arrivals, and on the day in question it left the port at 2.38pm. This put it at Staplehurst at 3.15pm, instead of 5.20pm as the foreman had anticipated.

If that was not bad enough, the train was doing in excess of 50mph as it travelled along the dead-straight section from Headcorn Station. At this speed the driver had little chance to react when he saw the lookout-signalman, who had been posted some 554 yards from the site of the p.w. work as opposed to the specified 1,000 yards. The train had slowed to about 30 mph when it reached the 'broken' track, but locomotive No.199's momentum carried it on over the break before it came to a halt on the west bank. Though some of the coaches remained upright, the bulk of the train crashed over the viaduct parapet dropping into the river below. In addition to the fatalities, forty other passengers sustained some form of injury. Dickens was particularly fortunate, his First-class coach being the one pictured here standing by itself on the viaduct.

Photograph Courtesy: Kent County Library

WATH (MR)
27 August 1887

In this volume of the series we shall meet a number of accidents caused by trains over-running signals two of which occurred on the Midland Railway in South Yorkshire. The first of these was at Wath-on-Dearne where a passenger train ran into the rear of a 33-wagon train as it was being shunted to allow the six-coach express to pass. When the leading draw-bar on the 22nd wagon broke, the Leeds-bound coal train became divided and a series of events began which led to 17 passengers and five railwaymen sustaining nasty injuries.

After the train had broken in two, the guard made a hand signal to the box, which the Wath Station signalman unfortunately took to mean that they had cleared the Manvers Main section and he sent the 'out of section' signal. Manvers Main then offered him the express, but he did not accept it and kept both his distant and home signals 'on'. As the crew of the coal train tried to re-couple the damaged private-owner wagon with a tail-rope, the express was leaving the Wath Road section at a speed of about 45 mph. Unfortunately, the driver of the express was not keeping a proper look-out, and as a consequence he over-ran the Manvers Main distant signal which had also been kept 'on'.

The driver of engine No. 51, was occupied in teaching a young passed-cleaner how to fire the engine, and he was not aware of the danger until the signalman shouted to him as he steamed past Manvers Main box. He got his steam-brake fully on and had put the engine into reverse as he slid past Wath distant signals, but it was too late to prevent the collision. The engine smashed through the brake van and the last coal truck, before mounting the next two vehicles. The spectacular results of the collision are captured in the photograph, though in view of the speed of the light-weight express it is very fortunate that no-one was killed. The express driver was clearly at fault, but the guard of the freight train was censured for not shunting his train earlier, the signalman and Station-master at Wath were criticised for not sending the 'obstruction danger' signal when the train became divided. The signalman at Manvers Main was reprimanded for accepting the express from Wath Road box, when he could clearly see that the coal train was standing on the main line.

National Railway Museum Photograph.

1366
VALE
VALE

HAMPTON WICK (LSWR)
6 August 1888

The Kingston Loop of the LSWR, which runs from New Malden Junction to Twickenham, had two intermediate junctions, a double one at Strawberry Hill where the Shepperton branch diverged, and another at Kingston for the goods depot. Just to the west of Kingston Junction the line crosses over the River Thames, after which it shortly enters the station at Hampton Wick. Just before midnight, on 6 August 1888 a signalman's error led to a 'light' engine, No. 484, being sent on the the wrong line from the junction to Twickenham. Running towards Kingston, bunker-first, was sister engine No. 486. Working the 10.50pm Down train from Waterloo, the 14-vehicle passenger train was just slowing down in preparation for its penultimate stop at Hampton Wick when the two bogie tank engines collided head-on at the north end of the station.

Both were badly damaged in the violent collision, the light engine being embedded under the bunker of the passenger train. The fireman of No. 486 was killed instantly and his driver was fatally injured, the passenger guard was seriously injured as was the driver of the light engine. The front five vehicles were badly damaged, claiming the lives of two passengers and seriously injuring 13 others. The leading coach, bird-cage brake van No. 96, mounted and telescoped into the following vehicle, Third-class coach No. 728. The next three were all composite carriages, No.s 2, 269, and 509, and all were extensively damaged.

The accident was attributed to four specific causes: 1, the primary cause was the signalman's error, which was then compounded by; 2, the lack of attention by the light engine crew who failed to notice they were on the wrong line; 3, poor signal installations at Kingston Junction; and finally, 4, the extreme length of time required to make the emergency bell-code as laid down in the L&SWR's signalling instruction. Though I do not normally quote direct from newspapers of the day, I felt that the report in the *Surrey Comet* provided an adequate example of the more than graphic comments that have had to be read as part of the research for this series. 'When the collision occurred the lamps in most of the carriages were extinguished, and the groans of the dying and injured, the screams of the terrified imprisoned passengers, and the hissing noise of the escaping steam all combined to form a ghastly and heart-rendering scene.'

Borough of Richmond on Thames Library Service.

PENISTONE (MS&LR)
30 March 1889

It is amazing how some locations have more than their fair share of disasters, and whilst one recognizes that this is a logical possibility at exceptionally busy junctions, it seems strange that some places appear to attract accidents like a magnet. One such location is Penistone, which has already had three accidents illustrated in this series (Volumes 1, 3, and 4). Only the accident in Volume 3 can be described as an attributable error, the other two are more in the line of freak occurrences. The same is true of the accident on 30 March 1889, when an excursion train was derailed because the leading axle of engine No. 188 fractured. An accident which claimed one passenger's life, and injury to 61 others.

Examination of the axle determined that there was a large crescent-shaped flaw at the left shoulder seat of the left wheel, and this flaw had grown in the 619,414 miles that the engine had run since it was built. Another, smaller, flaw was found on the shoulder seat of the right wheel. This could have been detected if the wheels had been removed at No. 188's previous overhaul, just three months earlier. The investigation revealed that the axle had failed, as the Up special from Liverpool/ Southport to King's Cross had left Dunford Bridge Station. Apparently the engine had been derailed then, but had rerailed itself on a set of trailing points. As No. 183 drew its train of 19 coaches through Huddersfield Junction at the east end of the station, an alert signalman in the junction box noted sparks coming from the front of the train and threw all his signals to danger.

The engine was pitched off the rails and 17 coaches were derailed, but the signalman's alert action helped the excursion train driver realize that something was badly wrong. In addition, by throwing all his signals to danger he prevented a Down mail train from running at speed into the wreckage. Though the mail train actually ran into the derailed coaches, its speed had been reduced sufficiently to ensure that this only resulted in minor damage. Ironically, several aspects of the report were identical to comments in the report on the 1884 accident at Penistone (which we covered in volume 4.), when a broken crank-axle caused a disastrous derailment near Bullhouse Colliery.

Photograph Courtesy: Barnsley Metropolitan Council Library & Archive Service

CHELFORD (LNWR)
22 December 1895

Passengers who travel on the former LNWR Manchester - Crewe line, may notice the small station of Chelford, roughly halfway between Stockport and Sandbach. Yet, the relatively quiet station of today conceals the awful tragedy which happened there almost a century ago. On 22 December 1895, the 4.15pm Up express left Manchester and headed towards Crewe in the face of a raging gale. It was made up of some 16 coaches, a mixture of 4-, 6- and 8-wheeled vehicles, drawn by a 2-4-0 'Jumbo' No.418 *Zygia* and No. 520 *Express,* a Webb split drive compound 2-2-2-0.

At the same time as the express approached Chelford, shunting operations were being carried out by a pick-up goods train on the Down side. In the course of the shunting, an empty wagon had been 'knocked back' on the Down main line, and this had come to halt some 162 yards away. Unfortunately, a sudden gust of wind started the wagon rolling back up the slight incline towards the point where the shunting was being carried out. The run-away then fouled a rake of wagons being pushed back into the siding, and was derailed on to the Up line. Despite the efforts of station staff, they were unable to warn the express and it hit the wagon at full speed, with the result that both engines were derailed.

Midway along the platform there was a small ramp, which gave access to the barrow crossing. The two year-old 'Jumbo' had the misfortune to run up it, and mounted the platform, where it smashed into the signal box before rolling over on to the Up line - badly injuring the footplate crew. *Express,* and the first four coaches, were derailed but remained upright. The next six coaches were all badly damaged, and the smashed remains were mixed up with the debris of the derailed wagons. This tragic accident was one which can be attributed to a caprice of nature, but nevertheless that sudden surge of wind accounted for the death of 14 passengers and occasioned injuries to 79 more.

National Railway Museum Photographs

CUDWORTH (MR)
19 January 1905

It would hardly seem possible that an experienced driver could run past no less than eight distant and five stop signals when they were all 'on', yet this is exactly what happened with a double-headed express train in the early hours of 19 January 1905. The result of this major driver-error, was a collision which claimed the lives of six passengers and the fireman of the leading engine. Though it was very foggy at the time, drivers of previous trains had all been able to see the signals, but only by running very slowly. The general rule book makes provision for the fact that signals may be obscured in bad weather, but makes no allowance for drivers running past them at danger. Consequently, if a driver could not read a signal, he was to treat it as being at danger, and not run past it at 50mph as happened in this case.

Taking in to account that the driver was entirely to blame, the duty of protecting signals in time of fog (or falling snow) also comes into question. In such conditions, fog-men are stationed at various signals, and being equipped with detonators and hand-lamps *(Rule 80),* they should be able to halt any train which over-ran a signal set at danger. At Cudworth, however, it would appear that the Midland Railway's abilities to comply with this rule were not all that they might have been. The fog-signalmen all lived some distance from their places of duty, the call-out man was sick (but had not reported this fact), his deputy did not know where some of the men lived, and detonators were not supplied to some of the fog-men. The BoT report was as critical of this aspect as it was of the driver, and suggested that the company should make provision for line-side housing for men employed in such duties, and the installation of telephone equipment in their cottages to facilitate a prompt call out. This was particularly essential in areas where fog was known to be common, such as at Cudworth. By strange coincidence I had to drive through the town on 19 January this year, and exactly the same conditions prevailed. And, even though I know the area well, I succeeded in driving past a Stop sign. Fortunately I was only going a few miles an hour and had ample time to avoid the other traffic, and was fortunately quite unlike the driver of the express some 85 years previously. *National Railway Museum Photograph.*

LIVERPOOL Hall Road (L&YR)
27 July 1905

In October 1904 the L&YR introduced a full electric service between Liverpool and Southport, which became the first main-line to convert from steam to electric traction. However, in view of the high acceleration that these electric trains attained, the *Railway Magazine* of September 1905 noted, 'High acceleration is far from an unmixed blessing'. This comment being brought about by an unusual accident that occurred at Hall Road, which was the terminal station for Liverpool suburban traffic. Once the last passengers had alighted, empty trains would pull out of the Down platform and run into a long carriage siding situated between the Up and Down main lines. In due course it would run through another set of points into the Up platform.

Though this arrangement was quite ingenious, it was flawed with having a set of facing-points on the Down main line. But, in order to ensure that through trains could not run into the siding, the point's switch-blades were inter-locked with the signal and, while ever the points were set for the siding, an electrical detector insured that the inner-home could not be lowered. Unfortunately, the points were some 200 yards from the box and it required a strong pull to move them.

On 27 July, the 6.20pm from Liverpool had just run into the siding, but the signalman was momentarily distracted and forgot to reset the points. So, when he tried to set the road for the 6.30pm express to Southport, the inner-home and the two distant signals remained at danger. Thinking there had been an equipment failure, and being anxious not to be reported for unnecessarily delaying an express he waved a green flag to the now near-stationary train. The motorman put on power and accelerated away. In the 350 yards from the signal to the toe of the facing point, the express got up to over 40 mph. When it was evident that the road was still set for the siding the motorman made a full brake application, but he skidded into the empty train some 50 yards further on. An eye witness stated that the rear coach of the local became detached from its trailing bogie (which was forced under the express) and its body shot into the air with the force of the impact. This then dropped onto the leading coach of the express causing the deaths of 21 passengers, and serious injuries to many others including the motorman.

Photographs Courtesy: B.C. Lane Collection

CHARING CROSS (SE&CR)
6 December 1905

In the events covered in this series we have, as the title implies, concentrated mostly on accidents to locomotives and rolling stock - however, there have also been some notable incidents relating to the failure of railway infra-structure. A specific example is recorded in the Board of Trade reports concerning a tragic accident at Charing Cross on 6 December 1905, when the station roof collapsed. Two men working on the roof at the time were killed instantly, and an employee of W.H. Smith & Son died later from injuries received when his kiosk was crushed. In addition, three workmen engaged on restoring the nearby Avenue Theatre were crushed to death by falling debris.

The station roof dated from 1863 and, like all roof structures under which steam engines (with their corrosive smoke emissions) passed, it was essential to ensure proper maintenance. On the day of the accident, a gang was at work, repairing, re-glazing and painting where required. About 3.30pm a loud noise was heard, and it was discovered that one of the tie-rods had snapped. No great significance was placed on this, but twelve minutes later two bays and the wind-screen at the river-end of the station completely collapsed. The roof had been fully over-hauled in 1898, and an inspection in 1902 had showed that both Charing Cross and Canon Street roofs were in good order. Work on the 1905 renewals began in June, and were largely completed by mid-November. By December only 20 men were still engaged on what was, effectively, the final phase. Unfortunately the collapse of the tie-rod, the weight of the workman's staging and scaffolding, and weak supporting abutments led to the collapse, which, in addition to the fatalities listed, occasioned eight other reported injuries. No passengers or rolling stock were harmed, but platforms 3 to 6 were put completely out of action for some considerable time.

Photograph Courtesy: Kent County Library Service

TONBRIDGE (SE&CR)
5 March 1909

If we are honest, most of us will admit that we hate being watched-over while we do our work - particularly so if the person doing the watching is in a position of superiority. The feelings this can engender are often worsened if the person is younger than us - for such is human nature! But, did such an element of human nature lead to a collision at Tonbridge Junction on 5 March 1909?

On the day in question, the Royal Train was due to convey King Edward VII to Dover, and it was booked to pass through Tonbridge Junction at 10.24 am. The timing had to be precise and, in order to ensure that no delays were experienced along the line, the Locomotive Superintendent issued instructions for preceding trains to carry an inspector to ensure punctuality. Two trains were schedule to pass through Tonbridge Junction before the 'Royal', these being the 'Continental Mail' which left Cannon St. at 9.05am, and an 8.30am fast train from Charing Cross to Dover. The booked times at Tonbridge being 9.50am and 9.55am respectively, but these trains were running slightly behind schedule and both approached the junction about 9.59am. The road was clear for the mail train, but when the fast-train passed Penshurst it was only allowed to work forward under Rule 5, as the section was clear but the junction was blocked.

However, all was not well aboard the footplate of 4-4-0 No. 497 as it made its way down to the junction. The right-hand feed pipe (situated under the foot-plate) was frozen and the fireman was trying to thaw it with burning tow, meanwhile steam from the chimney beat down on the boiler casing obscuring the driver's view. But the real problems seem to have been caused by an acronism between the 45-year old driver and the assistant loco. inspector who was only 24. Regretfully, neither the fireman or the inspector survived the crash, so only the driver's testimony remains as to what actually happened. He claimed that he was worried and over anxious to make up time due to adverse comments which the younger man had sniped continuously after leaving London. Whatever the case, it remained the driver's responsibility for observing signals, and he ran straight through the junction and smashed into the side of the 9-coach mail train drawn by 4-4-0 No. 165. The two fatalities were probably a result of the inspector and fireman jumping off the footplate immediately prior to the collision, but otherwise there were only a few very slight injuries. However, even though the consequences were not as severe as they might have been - the incident does bring into question the need for the presence of a third man on the footplate.

Photograph Courtesy: Kent County Library Service

WILLESDEN (LNWR)
5 December 1910

Though it is essential to examine the cause of serious accidents, it is also often very interesting to look at the speed with which rescue work was effected and normal services resumed. Accordingly I have concentrated on the events which took place at Willesden Junction on 5 December 1910 after a terrible rear-end collision occurred between two trains from Watford. Briefly, the accident was again another case of human error, resulting in the 8.30am train to Broad Street dashing into the back of the crowded 8.16am to Euston as it was standing in the station. The rear carriage of the stationary train was hit with considerable force and splinters of glass and wood showered platforms three and four. The roof was detached and fell down on top of the next coach into which the body had been telescoped. Both these then coaches tipped over against the side of the platform, but were prevented from falling right over by the stone edges. The next two coaches were also badly damaged, but all the passengers managed to get out through the doors.

Three people were killed and over forty others were injured - some quite seriously. However, the toll may have been even higher had it not been for the superb efforts of the rescuers. Railwaymen have had a long tradition in first-aid, and at Willesden Junction their skills were fully utilized. Pieces of shattered woodwork were used as splints, whilst carriage seats were torn out and improvised as stretchers. A Mrs. Ginger who assisted in the station buffet managed to extract a large bottle of brandy from the bar, and passed among the injured asking them 'if they would like a little something to steady their nerves!' Men from the engine sheds quickly arrived on the scene with heavier tools, whilst a breakdown train was made ready. The manager at the nearby Bedford Motor Company's works sent a fleet of vehicles to help convey the wounded to hospital, whilst several local doctors made their way to render assistance on the scene. One of the curious things about the accident, is the number of people who climbed onto the top of the carriages to render assistance, one man even made his way onto the damaged roof of the rear coach, but fellow rescuers urged to him to get down quickly when they saw how precariously balanced it was. Obviously Willesden was a major junction, and it was essential that the running lines be cleared at the earliest opportunity. The breakdown gang had arrived about 10am, just over an hour after the crash, and by three pm almost all traces of the disaster (apart from the broken platform edges) had been completely removed. Therefore it is little wonder that photographs of this accident have been very hard to come by.

Photograph Courtesy: London Borough Of Brent

PONTYPRIDD (TVR)
23 January 1911

In Trains In Trouble we have seen a number of accidents which occurred when a signalman forgot about a train in his section, and then allowed another one to enter it. Though there are many reasons for such aberrations, the Associated Railway Companies Rule Book, had a very good safeguard to ensure these mistakes did not lead to an accident. This rule, No.55, required any driver standing at a signal for more than three minutes (or immediately if visibility was bad), to send his fireman to advise the signalman of their position.

On 23 January 1911, an 0-6-2T, No.121, working a Hafod - Barry coal train came to a halt at the outer-home signal of Rhondda Cutting Box near Pontypridd Coke Ovens. Instead of applying the fundamental *Rule No.55,* the driver whistled for a signal, and then sent his mate to fill the engine's lubricators. Accordingly it was some 12 minutes before the fireman walked into the cabin to tell the signalman of their presence on No. 1 road. The signalman could not believe his ears, for he said he had no knowledge of the train being in his section at all. It took him between 30 and 60 seconds to comprehend what was being said, but he then sent the 'blocking back' signal as he had already accepted a passenger train from Gyfeillon Signal Box. The BoT inspector concluded it was hard to understand how two experienced signalmen had made the mistake of 'losing' the freight train, but put it down to their irregular working of the Tyer's two-position single wire block telegraph instruments. Whatever the case, the 9.15am passenger train from Treherbert to Cardiff, headed by 0-6-2T No. 193 ran into the back of the standing train at a speed between 25 and 30 mph. The coal train's brake van, No.6361, was completely demolished and the guard was seriously injured, dying in Cardiff Infirmary some weeks later. In addition to this fatality, eleven passengers were killed and four more seriously injured.
Topham Picture Library.

RAMSGATE TOWN (SE&CR)
11 March 1913

In our look at less-serious accidents, an unusual occurrence was noted in the spring of 1913, when a run-away train collided with a brake van standing at the buffer stops in Ramsgate Town Station. The train was the 1.55pm up passenger train from Margate Sands Station to Ashford, reversing at Ramsgate. The engine, a Wainwright H class 0-4-4T, No. 324, worked into Margate Sands Station at 1.02pm with a three-coach train of bogie stock from Canterbury. On arriving here, the driver was informed that a 6-wheeled brake-van, No.681, was to be attached for through-working to London. The three coaches were detached, and the van marshalled in behind the engine before the train was coupled up by the duty carriage-shunter.

It was normal practice to first attend to the screw-link coupling, then join up the vacuum brake-pipes, followed by the steam-heating pipes. But, on this occasion, the shunter found the steam-heating pipe was burning his leg whilst he dealt with the coupling, so he attended to this next. Having taken this task out of sequence, his attention was diverted and he routinely climbed back on to the platform - leaving the brake-pipes un-connected. Though the train stood at the platform for about 20 minutes, the omission was not only over-looked by the shunter, but also the driver, guard and station inspector. The train duly set out on time for the 3-mile run to Ramsgate - unknown to all, that the only operative brakes were those on the engine. As per local practice, the guard was riding in the brake van behind the engine, and not in the rear coach as prescribed in the rule book. On approaching Ramsgate the driver tried to apply his brakes, but the combined weight of the train, some 98 tons 15 cwt, pushed him into No. 1 platform at about 8mph. The van at the end of this road was knocked through the buffer stops, onto the platform and, as the lower right picture shows, through the entrance doors.

Nine passengers were slightly injured, and a young girl entering the station was badly bruised by falling bricks. The report noted that the locomotive (seen below left) collided with the van, because the percentage of un-braked to total rolling weight was as high as 72%. The final words on this accident should rightly go to Major J.W. Pringle, the investigating officer, who said: 'It seems hardly possible that a case of this sort should happen, where four men are responsible for the proper connection of brake pipes.'

Photographs Courtesy: Kent County Library Service

ILFORD (GER)
1 January 1915

In terms of sheer numbers of injuries sustained by passengers, the collision which occurred at Ilford Station on 1 January 1915 has to rank as one of the most serious. Only ten people lost their lives, but over 500 passengers notified the company of injuries or shock sustained when an express passenger train ran into the side of a local train.

New Year's Day 1915 was just an ordinary working day, and in common with many other services on the GER during the first winter of World War One, it was very much business as usual at Ilford Station. About 8.40am a local train from Gidea Park to Liverpool Street Station, which ran non-stop after Seven Kings, was allowed on to the Up through line in precedence to the 7.06am express passenger train from Clacton to London. The 2-4-2T was just drawing its train of 18 4-wheeled carriages across from the Up local line, when 4-4-0 No.1813 over-ran the signals and ploughed into the side of the seventh coach practically destroying it. The cause was in part attributed to smoke hanging round the express engine's boiler obscuring the signals, but was primarily due to the driver completely missing the home signal. Though he claims to have seen it at the last minute, and made an emergency brake application, the inspector concluded it had only been the explosion of two fog detonators that had alerted him to the fact that he had passed the signal at danger. As a consequence he had less than 120 yards to bring his train to a halt, whereas if the emergency-detonator placing equipment had been installed at the distant signal, he would have had some 770 yards in which to stop. Though the driver was clearly at fault, the omission of providing an audible warning when a distant signal was passed at danger was once again brought into question. Regretfully, the warning (though repeated again and again) was not fully heeded on Britain's railways until well after nationalization - of the pre-grouped and grouped railways, only the GWR fully developed this form of protection with its invaluable A.W.S. system.

Photograph Courtesy: Topham Picture Library

SMITHY BRIDGE (L&YR)
18 March 1915

In discussing Cudworth, we have touched on the rule concerning the observance of signals during fog or falling snow, and noted the consequences when a driver failed to treat unseen signals as though they were standing at danger. A similar occurrence took place on the L&YR's trans-Pennine route, a few miles south of Summit in March 1915, when the experienced driver of a Leeds/Bradford - Fleetwood express ran into the back of a stationary train.

With the snow creating difficulties like frozen points and minor derailments, traffic had been building up all evening on the west side of the Pennines. So, when the 4.49pm empty stock train from Normanton to Red Bank arrived at Smithy Bridge at 8.25pm, the signalman had to hold it on the main line as all the available siding accommodation was fully occupied. According to *Rule 55,* the fireman went at once to inform the signalman of their presence. The signalman, also playing things exactly to the book, set all his signals to danger behind the standing train.

Quite why the driver of the Atlantic 4-4-0, No. 1394, passed all the signals at danger is something of a mystery. It is possible that the falling snow may have obscured his view, for it had 'blanked out' the spectacle plates at the front of the locomotive. The alternative was for the driver to put his head round the side of the cab to watch for the signals, which would have been both a difficult and unpleasant task. It is inconceivable that a man with the character and experience of this driver would have deliberately over-run signals at a speed of 40 to 45mph, and one must conclude that he had not seen them. Obviously the same comment applied here as it did at Cudworth, in that the driver should not have taken it for granted that even a principle express train would have a clear road. The driver and three passengers lost their lives, and 33 people were injured.

Once again the need for an A.W.S. system was raised in the report, which said: 'This unfortunate collision is another case which points to the desirability of the provision of some arrangement for giving the driver an unmistakable warning as to the position of the Distant signal when he passes it.'

Photograph Courtesy: Metro Rochdale, Rochdale Central Library.

WEEDON (LNWR)
14 August 1915

Our trio of serious accidents during 1915 concludes with an unfortunate incident that led to the derailment of the Irish Mail train, which in turn caused the deaths of 10 passengers and injuries to 64 other persons. The accident was due to the failure of a split-pin on a George the Fifth Class 4-4-0, which was working the 8.45am Up express from Birmingham New Street to Euston.

On Saturday 14 August 1915, in the second year of World War I, No. 1489 *Wolfhound* left Monument Lane shed at 8.10am in readiness for its run to the capital. The trip was uneventful as far as Rugby, but as the driver oiled round his locomotive whilst they waited in the station, he noticed that a split-pin was missing from the right-hand driving crank-pin washer. A fitter was summoned to assist, and rather than delay the train, he removed a similar pin from engine No. 665 standing nearby. The exchange took about four minutes, and the Euston train left on time. However, somewhere after leaving Rugby the pin became detached and the washer followed suit as the train passed through Weedon Station at about 60mph. The loss of the pin and washer allowed the locking collar to un-screw itself causing the coupling rod to come off the driving crank-pin. However as the rod was still attached to the trailing crank-pin, it flailed round and round destroying the Down track. The Euston train was brought to a halt near Stowe Hill tunnel, and the crew followed correct procedures for protecting the standing train.

Unfortunately, it had not occurred to the driver that his broken coupling rod had damaged the other track, so he gave no thought to the danger which lay in wait for the mail train. Headed by a 4-4-0 Precedent Class, No. 1189 *Stewart,* and a Renown Class 4-4-0, No 1971 *Aurora,* the 15-coach Irish Mail hit the damaged track and was derailed at high speed. The circumstances of this accident were of an unusual character, but coupled with events at Quintinshill and St. Bede's Junction, in addition to those covered in this book, Weedon helped make 1915 the worst year in the history of British railways. Tragically, the same place was attended by a further unusual mechanical failure on 21 September 1951 when No. 46207 *Princess Arthur of Connaught* was derailed at high speed due to incorrect maintenance.
Topham Picture Library

RATHO (NBR)
3 January 1917

In the vast majority of accident reports we encounter that most understandable of causes, human error, where a momentary lapse led to disaster. Occasionally, we find accidents caused by individuals deliberately flouting the rules, but rarely do we see rules persistently being broken by a large number of railway personnel. Yet, such a situation was noted at Ratho, where an incorrect operating procedure had developed in connection with the empty stock trains on the Queensferry Branch. Near the junction, the single-track branch split into two loops, and the train would run into the Down loop where it detached the stock. The engine then ran 'light' on to the Down-main, crossed to the Up-main, before coming back through the Up loop on to the single track, this accomplished it would reverse back onto the other end of the train standing in the Down loop. This unusual procedure involved the 'light' engine running in a facing direction on both main lines which, of course, was asking for trouble. There had been a major collision at the junction just over five years earlier, this was put down to a misunderstanding between the

driver of a goods engine and the signalman. Yet, two or three other later incidents also appear to show that irregular working was causing near-misses. Such problems were to soon be compounded by the greater use of the Queensferry Branch, brought about by the 1914-18 War (see Railways At War Vol.2).
On the afternoon of 3 January a 4-4-0, No. 421 *Jingling Geordie,* came up the branch with an empty stock train, and the signalman noticed the crew begin to detach the coaches. However, he kept his branch signals 'on', because he had just accepted a Down express from Edinburgh. But, to his horror, as the 4-4-2 No. 874 *Dunedin* approached the junction, No. 421 burst through the points at the end of the Down loop. As trap-points were only installed on the Up loop, it ran un-hindered to the main line. Running in a facing direction tender first, No. 421 struck *Dunedin* head-on. The goods engine's tender was completely wrecked by the impact, and the front end was badly damaged as it was driven forward by the force of the No.874. The express was fully loaded and 12 passengers were killed as the front coach completely broke up. A magnificent job of rescue work was undertaken by servicemen travelling on the express, but 44 people were badly hurt, including both drivers. Colonel Pringle's report observed that this accident had only occurred due to this irregular turning of trains on the wrong road, and it was at once stopped by the NBR's traffic superintendent. However, it must be said that it seems incredible that such a practice could have gone on for so long without it being brought to management's attention.
NBR Official Photographs, Courtesy: Scottish Record Office

Frome and the first two coaches forced their way past the debris and came to a stand on the opposite side, but the third and fourth coaches parted company and piled up around the bridge. Pullman car *Carmen* was thrown across the track, but the superior carriage design employed by Pullman ensured that damage to it was limited.

Thirteen passengers were killed and 21 others were seriously injured, but the sturdy construction of the locomotive saved the lives of the driver and his 'mate'. The River Class were all withdrawn and converted into tender engines as a result of this accident, but before this work was completed one of the class was tested on the former GNR section of the LNER. I am indebted to two readers who were involved in these tests with the late H.N. Gresley, for the detailed notes forwarded after volume five was published - these show that the River Class was capable of speeds in excess of 85mph on a good road - hopefully this information will form the basis for a future article.

Photographs Courtesy: Kent County Library Service

SEVENOAKS (SR)
24 August 1927

In Volume 5 we discussed the accident at Bearstead that occurred on 22 August 1927, involving a 2-6-4T No. 800 *River Frome* which was derailed because of imperfections in the track. However as events of two days later were to show, it was not just poor track that was involved, for the class were particularly sensitive to bad sections of the 'road', which caused them to rock and sway at speeds of between 50 and 60mph. Most drivers knew about the tendency of water to swish around in the side tanks, so to prevent this surging they would put on coal and reverse the dampers. On 24 August, the 5pm Cannon Street to Folkestone, comprised of No. 800, seven coaches and a Pullman car, was emerging from Polhill Tunnel at about 57mph when the driver adopted this tactic. However, between Dunton Green and Sevenoaks a knocking noise was heard at the front end of the engine and he shut off the regulator.

The noise was the sound of the flanges on the leading-bogie wheels hitting the rail chairs, so the driver braked hard, knowing there was a set of catch-points just ahead, close to an over-line bridge. Unfortunately, the derailed engine slammed into the central pier of Shoreham Bridge, and being made of concrete the support was completely smashed. *River*

DINWOODIE (LMS)
25 October 1928

About 3am on the morning of 25 October, the Down 'Royal Highlander' express from Euston to Aberdeen and Inverness was passing between Wamphray and Dinwoodie when it quite literally ran into trouble. For, the signalman at Wamphray (who had been experiencing problems at home due to the ill-health of his wife and young baby) had got into the habit of falling asleep at his post. Being awakened by the bell-code signals for the express, he had cleared the 'boards' without having ensured that the preceding 35-vehicle freight train had left his section. Accordingly, the double-headed express was allowed to proceed under clear signals and whilst travelling at about 60 mph, it struck the back of the freight train which had come to a stand due to a mechanical defect. Unfortunately, the guard of the Carlisle to Dundee working had not been as efficient as he should have been, and it was almost a full 15 minutes before he

began laying detonators to protect the train's rear end, by which time it was too late!

The express train's pilot engine an ex-Caledonian 4-4-0, No. 14435, went through the 20 ton brake van at floor level, completely demolishing it. In turn, the van's heavy ballast blocks ripped away the pilot engine's bogie and a good deal of the under-gear. It rolled over and ploughed down the side of the embankment, followed by the train engine, a standard compound 4-4-0 No. 1176. All four enginemen were killed instantly, but due to the sturdiness of the coaching stock only five passengers suffered from slight injuries or shock. Though the accompanying pictures show a great deal of damage to the two leading vehicles, the all-steel construction prevented wide-spread injury and probably saved many lives. As a result of Dinwoodie, the Ministry of Transport recommended that where all-steel vehicles were included in a train, they should be marshalled next to the engine to prevent telescoping. However, in practice this rarely happened unless such a vehicle just happened to be at the right end of the train. Therefore, in a large number of subsequent accident reports we read of telescoped wooden-bodied vehicles which had been placed next to the locomotive when all-steel stock was marshalled elsewhere in the train. *Upper: Ken Longbottom Collection. Lower: Barr Collection: Glasgow Transport Museum.*

DOE HILL (LMS)
12 February 1929

On 12 February 1929, yet another disastrous collision befell an LMS express in the early hours of the morning. In order to allow a fast train to pass, an express freight train was shunted from the Up-goods line to the Up-passenger at Morton Sidings signal box, which was located roughly mid-way between Clay Cross and Alfreton. However, when the signalman gave the 'right away', he had erroneously re-started the 10.50pm from Sheffield to Birmingham Soho on the wrong line. This section of the former Midland Railway had four running lines, and though they knew they had to go through the cross-over at Morton Sidings after the shunt, neither the driver nor his fireman realized they had not done so. The class 4F 0-6-0, No. 4491, was thus allowed to proceed southwards on the Down passenger line with its train of 34 goods wagons and a 20-ton brake van. In fact the error went un-noticed until they reached Doe Hill Station where, upon observing that the platforms were on his wrong side, the driver brought the train to a stand. On doing this he sent his fireman to change the head-lamps to show a red aspect and then set off to lay detonators, but as he walked down the track he saw the head-lamps of an approaching express - the 9.30pm from St. Pancras to Glasgow.

Running at about 40mph at the head of a thirteen-coach train, was No. 5977 a standard four-cylinder Claughton 4-6-0. The express driver had no chance of avoiding the collision, and both he and his mate were killed instantly in the impact. The first two vehicles in the train were wooden bodied, both telescoped into each other and were totally wrecked, part of the body on the first one was thrown thirty feet to the west of the frame. The third vehicle was of all-steel construction and had been built in 1927, though almost completely destroyed it absorbed a lot of the lateral-force. As a result the three all-steel bogie brake vans which followed, no.s 7067, 7352, and 7969, were all derailed, but with lessening degrees of damage. The remainder of the train was un-damaged, and afterwards was able to go forward.

A few passengers were thrown from their seats in the sixth vehicle, corridor composite No. 9328, but the 12-wheel sleeping car which came next was hardly shaken - in fact one passenger slept throughout the whole incident and, when woken the following morning, was astonished to hear of the proceedings. Though a signalman's error and a lack of attention by the footplate crew of No. 4491 led to this disaster, it is a remarkably interesting accident because it emphasized exactly what Colonel A.H.L. Mount had tried to bring home about the correct marshalling of all-steel vehicles after the tragedy at Dinwoodie!

National Railway Museum Photographs

LITTLE SALKELD (LMS)
10 July 1933

Our next accident is quite unique, because (as far as I have been able to discover) 4-4-0 No.1010 is the only locomotive ever to have been involved in two separate serious accidents at exactly the same location - Little Salkeld. In the first instance the engine was derailed by a landslip on 19 January 1918, and on the second occasion, 10 July 1933, the collision was due to human-error. Little Salkeld was one of the small-type stations on the Settle-Carlisle line, and the signal box was equipped with one of the smaller Midland frames. The box was not continuously manned, and was only 'switched in' when a train had to be set back to allow an express to pass, or when wagons were being dropped off in the yard. Therefore, it was operated by a passed-porter and, according to the report, the man doing the job in 1933 was not a very good one. That day he had knocked off an hour early to take his lunch at 12.30pm, because a Down freight train which usually passed at 1.30pm sometimes had a wagon to drop off. He was just having his lunch when the freight train arrived 25 minutes early, and in something of a temper he left his lodgings to attend to it.

Sure enough, the freight had a single wagon of coal to drop, and he had to open up the box. However, he did not first check the traffic position with the adjacent boxes at Langwathby and Lazonby, before moving the inter-locked points which also threw the Home signals to danger. The crew of the freight uncoupled the train behind the third wagon, and the class 4F 0-6-0, No. 4091 ran forward, before being signalled to push the wagons over the cross-over onto the Up line. At that moment the Up Thames-Forth express, came rushing out of Long Meg cutting under clear distant signals at around 60mph. The compound hit the leading wagon which was just fouling the Up line, and then smashed into the tender of the 4F. Number 1010 was derailed to the left and ran on along a paved cartway in the goods yard, coming to rest 90 yards further on. Its coaches scraped though the wreckage and many had their sides ripped open, causing injuries to about half of the 60 passengers on board. The fireman of No.1010 was seriously injured, but the 4F's driver was fatally injured. The 'signalman' later claimed he thought that the express had passed during his lunch but, as it was not due to leave Carlisle until 12.44pm, he had most likely forgotten all about it.

National Railway Museum Photographs

GLASGOW (LMS)
6 September 1934

The accident at Port Eglington Junction on 6 September 1934 is remarkable in that it has revealed photographs of an LMS class 2P 4-4-0, No. 639, which was previously thought to be one of the few members of the class to elude the camera's lens. It is also of interest, because the collision occurred after a period of almost a year's immunity from passenger fatality in train accidents, which had thus far been one of the longest periods so recorded in British railway history. Sadly, that evening was to claim the lives of three footplatemen and six passengers, whilst one driver and 10 passengers were seriously injured. Eighteen more passengers and both guards were detained in hospital, and a further 27 others reported injuries of various kinds.

Number 639, was working a 6-coach Glasgow (St. Enoch) - Kilmarnock train, when it was hit head-on by sister loco. No. 591 on a Paisley - St. Enoch train with a similar number of bogies. The Kilmarnock train thus weighed 233 tons, whilst the Paisley train was probably about 257 tons. Only the driver of the Paisley train survived and, though seriously injured, it was his evidence that provided the central point of reference for the accident investigators.

The driver said that as he had pulled away from Shields Road Station he noted the junction signals were off. He was running tender first, and had to turn round to 'notch-up' the regulator, however he claimed the home signals were reversed and when he next looked up they were showing danger. He had no chance of touching the reversing gear, and judged that he had got to a speed of 20mp when he realized the situation. The engine was then little more than 165 yards from the point of collision, and No. 591 was heading towards them at a speed of between 25 and 30 mph. Colonel Mount thoroughly examined the situation at Port Eglington, both in the signal box and by twice riding on the footplate of a 4-4-0 running tender-first.

For the trains to have met when they did, and at the speeds at which they were running, the home signal could not have been clear 40 seconds after No. 591 left Shields Road. Even though it would have been possible for the signalmen to have reversed the signals in 29 seconds, Colonel Mount concluded that the driver had actually seen another set of signals and was thus misled. He commented, 'I noted myself how deceptive these signals might be, and, as stated, there was unnecessary obscuration of [signals] No. 73/75 which I understand has since been dealt with. ......The circumstances of this collision illustrate the necessity for safeguarding the fallibility of drivers in respect of junction operation.' With semaphore installation at the junction it was difficult to improve the position, but had the St. Enoch colour-light signalling system been extended as far as this extremely busy junction, the accident would probably have been preventable. There was also a question of irregular operation of a signalling system which could allow three trains in the same section at

the same time, no matter how long this method of operation had been worked on the basis of Regulation No. 4. The company therefore came in for a degree of criticism, and were advised to apply standard instructions for junction block working. The luckless driver was tried on a charge of culpable homicide before a Sheriff and Jury in Glasgow on 28 January 1935. The trial lasted three days, but in the end the jury returned a unanimous 'Not Guilty' verdict and he was acquitted.

Picture Left. The scene at Port Eglington shortly after the collision, with the tender of No. 591 pressed hard into the side of No 639, behind which can be seen the wreckage of the two leading coaches in the Kilmarnock Train. Third-brake No. 24350 and Third-class No. 17483, both of which had wooden bodies and underframes.

Picture Upper-right: Class 2P 4-4-0 No, 591 after the collision, separated from its tender which understandably suffered the worst of the damage in the Paisley train.

Picture Lower-right: No. 639 after recovery, but minus its bogie truck. As can be seen, the engine was seriously damaged in the collision, and the boiler and frames were judged as being beyond repair.

All Courtesy: Barr Collection, Glasgow Museums

SLEAFORD (LNER)
15 February 1937

The accidents on this page could almost be captioned 'Coaches In Trouble', for these two Lincolnshire derailments both resulted in heavy damage to the rolling stock. On 15 February 1937 a group of five platelayers had just 'knocked-off' for their lunch and retired to a cabin alongside Sleaford North Junction on the Lincoln - Spalding line, when a York - Lowestoft express passing through the junction became derailed. Three of the leading coaches broke away from the train and, being diverted to the left, two of these ran over the p.w. cabin, killing three of the gang instantly. A fourth man died in hospital later that evening and the fifth was seriously injured.

It would appear that the experienced driver of LNER class B17, No. 2829 *Narworth Castle* had over-estimated the degree of reduction of speed at Sleaford North distant signals and, instead of negotiating the junction at the prescribed maximum of 20mph, the accident inspector concluded that it must have been in the neighbourhood of 40mph. In view of the fact that the 10 coach train was well loaded, it is perhaps fortunate that only 15 minor cases of injuries and shock resulted among the passengers.
Eltham-Chronicle Collection

LANGRICK (LNER)
8 March 1937

Just three weeks after the Sleaford accident, and only twelve miles to the west, there was another lunch-time derailment on the LNER. Whilst working the 12.44pm Boston - Lincoln express, class K3 2-6-0, No. 126 split the rails at 40 mph and left the track. The train, comprised of a quad-art non-corridor set, a 6-wheeled brake van and a 6-wheeled Third-class saloon, forced its way past the tender causing the damage shown opposite.

The investigation into the accident laid the blame on the condition of the permanent-way - in particular the condition of the sleepers, of which 68% dated from when the GNR had first laid the track in 1895. In 1931 it was proposed that this complete section should be re-laid the following year, but head-office deferred the request, and apparently the matter was forgotten. The final straw came when the class K3s began working regular turns on the line, for these heavy, rigid locomotives were particularly hard on the track. In fact, only the previous July, K3 class No.2764 had been involved in the serious accident at Postland a few miles south-east of Spalding.
Atlantic Collection

NEWPORT (GWR)
19 August 1938

Any examination of accident statistics will reveal a significantly low number of serious incidents being reported on the Great Western Railway which, it must be said, had the finest safety record of any of the 'big four'. Its signalling and train control systems all being developed with absolute safety in mind. However, even though the company had done all it could to minimise the risk of accidents, there was still the element of human error to contend with. By way of example I have chosen this incident at Newport, Monmouthshire, on 19 August 1938 which, although it only resulted in minor injuries to three passengers, was potentially one of the most disastrous ever experienced by the GWR.

The train involved was an express from Crewe which divided into two sections for Bristol and Cardiff at Newport. It was the rear section of this train, the 11.54pm to Bristol, which was involved in the accident. It was some 16 minutes late when the 4-6-0 49xx class engine, No 4925 *Eynsham Hall* backed down onto the train. The driver was on the right hand side of the engine, and he incorrectly allowed his fireman to read the disc signals on the left hand side of the train as he could not see them. If he had not been too anxious to get his train away (in order to meet a guaranteed London connection at Bristol), he could have crossed to that side of the engine to check the signals for himself. Unfortunately, this error compounded a mistake which had already been made by the signalman, who had pulled off the wrong levers. Though the signals showed a green light, the road was actually set for a release siding at the east end of the station. This short spur actually led to a stop-block which was adjacent to the parapet of the bridge over the flooded River Usk, and if the fireman had not been observant, the engine would have ploughed through the buffers and dived into the river below. Fortunately, the man redeemed his earlier mistake by seeing the red light on the stop-block and shouted for his driver to brake. As it was, the force of the impact tore apart the fishing of the last rail joint and forced the buffer stop forward, with the train only coming to a halt when its buffers struck the bridge parapet.
Atlantic Collection

HAROLD WOOD (LNER)
10 February 1941

In February 1941, during the dark days of World War II, another tragedy struck the railways when a Southend train collided with the rear of a Norwich Express which had come to halt in mid-section. In those days, the trains were heavily loaded and the 13-coach express to Norwich was no exception when it drew out of Liverpool Street at 10am behind a Class B17. Though these 4-6-0s were the most powerful engines in use on the Great Eastern section at that time, No. 2828 *Harewood House* was unable to ascend the 1 in 100 bank between Harold Wood and Brentwood due to its weight and a consequent lack of steam. It was still standing there when a Class B12 4-6-0, No. 8556, under full steam ran into the back of it at 30mph.

The Norwich train was pushed forwards about 20 yards, with the last vehicle (a wooden-bodied brake 2nd) being completely destroyed. The B12 literally tore through it, with the roof coming down on the engine's boiler casing as the accompanying pictures clearly show. Seven lives were claimed as a result, and 17 more were seriously injured, though the rest of the train escaped with only minimal damage. The front two coaches on the Southend train telescoped, but there were no injuries as the first vehicle, a brake third, and the first three compartments at the leading end of the next coach were empty.

At the time of this accident, much of the line from Liverpool Street to Shenfield and Southend had been equipped with colour-light signalling, though there were one or two notable exceptions which we will discuss later. When the driver of the B17 brought his train to a stand, he did so by colour-light signal DT17 and used its telephone to advise the signalman. In addition, because the Norwich train had not cleared the track-circuit, the automatic controls kept signal DT16B behind it at danger, and had signal DT16 showing a yellow aspect. Why the driver of the B12 over-ran these two signals in good visibility is unknown, but the investigating officer concluded that he must have fallen asleep and missed seeing them. If the guard of the Norwich train had managed to lay detonators 200 yards back down the line instead of just 30 yards, the explosions may have warned the crew of the B12 and roused the driver in order for him to take preventative action. Once again, this showed the need for Automatic Train Control, which would have provided an audible warning when a signal was over-run.

Lower Left: Stratford Depot's, Ransomes & Rapier crane begins work on clearing the wreckage. Atlantic Collection

Lower Right: Showing the roof of the rear coach adorning the boiler of the B12, while police and railwaymen look on. Eltham Times Collection

FERRYHILL (LNER)
5 January 1946

Just north of Ferryhill there is a sharp dip with falling gradients on either side, where the East Coast Main Line descends to cross the River Browney on its way to Durham. On the morning of 5 January 1946 this dip provided the ideal conditions for the rear-portion of a divided goods train to over-take the front section. As a result of the ensuing collision, the debris of 14 wagons was thrown onto the adjacent line. The goods train was running from Low Fell to Doncaster, and was made up of 44 4-wheeled wagons, a 20-ton brake van and Class B16 4-6-0 No.842. As the driver approached Bridge House signal box, about 5.30am, he noticed the Up Home signal at danger and slowed down to walking pace as a signalman was standing by the track. The man was going on duty at Ferryhill, and had been authorized to get a lift on this freight. As he got on the footplate he felt a slight jerk, and joked to the driver 'that he hoped he hadn't divided the train'. He had, for the snatch caused when the driver released his brake had broken a dangerously weak draw-bar on the seventh wagon from the engine (ex-L&YR 1 plank wagon No.147330).

The signalman saw the division and notified the next box at Browney, the man there could have let the front half of the train run on to the Hett Mill section, but was fearful that by doing so he might cause a derailment on Croxdale Viaduct. Accordingly, he brought the B16 to a halt in the protection of his box, and put 'on' his Down Home signal to safeguard the 11.15pm King's Cross - Newcastle express which was due. Unfortunately, no-one was to know that when the collision occurred, a portion of one of the wagons would slip down the embankment and catch the signal wires leading out of the box, pulling both the Down Home and Down Distant signals 'off'. The crew of the Class V2, 2-6-2 No. 4895 were therefore misled as to the state of the line, so at about 50mph they ran headlong into the wreckage. Ten passengers were killed and eight were badly hurt in what turned out to be 'Britain's Black Week On The Railways', when three fatal accidents occurred - including the major disaster at Lichfield where 20 lives were lost.
Atlantic Collection

GIDEA PARK (LNER)
2 January 1947

When I first read this accident report, I thought it sounded all too familiar. The ingredients were very much the same as Cudworth, Smithy Bridge, and a whole host of other incidents where unseen signals were over-run during a period of bad visibility. We have already noted the often repeated suggestions of the Railway Inspectorate, recommending the need for Automatic Train Control or Advance Warning Systems, and you are justified in asking why a reliable system was not universally introduced. Likewise, the need for colour-light signalling to replace semaphore signals, with their dim oil lights, had been clearly demonstrated in a number of cases where fog was involved.

Almost certainly, the provision of high intensity colour-lights, with a system of audible warning, would have prevented the terrible rear-end collision at Gidea Park, on 2 January 1947. Yet, the absence of such safety measures, coupled with failures in manual fog signalling, meant that there was no other warning for a driver who had missed seeing that the semaphore signals were set at danger. His train, the 10.25pm to Peterborough drawn by class B17 4-6-0, No. 1602 *Walsingham,* had been dislocated by the fog and having lost its 'path', left Liverpool Street some 25 minutes late. The preceding train was the 10.28pm to Southend, headed by Class B12 4-6-0. No. 1565 left Liverpool St. on schedule, but by the time Gidea Park Station was reached it had dropped 16 minutes due to the fog. It was just starting away from the station, when the express passed the distant and home signals at danger and, at a speed of about 33mph, buried itself into the back of the slow moving train. The express train's coaches were fitted with buck-eye couplings, and thus telescoping and serious damage was prevented. Unfortunately, the three rear coaches of the Southend train were completely wrecked, and five passengers were killed outright, with two more receiving fatal injuries, a further 45 people were detained in hospital. The accompanying pictures clearly show the fate of the train, though the damage to the station was only superficial.

In a way it is unfair to criticise the LNER for still operating with semaphore signals in the case of this tragedy, for a planned colour-light scheme along this part of the line had been postponed on the outbreak of World War II. Yet, even these new signals were not totally fool-proof as had been shown by an accident just three years earlier at nearby Ilford, when nine people were killed after a danger signal was missed in dense fog.

Pictures: Atlantic Collection

SOUTH CROYDON (SR)
24 October 1947

The incidence of accidents involving older EMU stock has been quite prominent in the media in recent years, but the phenomena is not a new one as we have already seen in this series. On the intensified suburban railway network where these units are employed, it is perhaps understandable that accidents will happen more often than on less busy lines - particularly when adverse conditions affect normal operation. Such was the case on 24 October 1947 when, once again, dense fog blanketed the countryside.

In the early morning rush hour, several trains making their way toward London were converging near the busy junctions at South Croydon. The first of these trains, from Tunbridge Wells, had been offered to South Croydon box at 8.21am, but the signalman did not accept it as he intended to give precedence to a train from Littlehampton. Accordingly, when Purley Oaks box offered an 8-car EMU, from Haywards Heath with 800 passengers on board (at 8.26), he declined it in order to allow the delayed Tunbridge train get away. Unfortunately the Haywards Heath train was forgotten by the Purley Oaks signalman who, having lost sight of it in the fog, then accepted a 9-car EMU from Tattenham Corner carrying over 1,000 passengers.

The inexperienced signalman, who was only a passed porter, was anxious not to delay traffic and pulled off his signals for the Tattenham Train. The Haywards Heath train saw the signals clear, and began to move slowly forward. This operated one of the treadles in Purley Oaks box, and if the signalman had taken notice of this warning this gave, the accident would have been averted. Unfortunately, he misled himself into believing that the treadle had failed (in fairness it should be said that he had experienced a number of similar failures in the past week), and as a result he used his release-key to reset the instruments without checking with the signalmen on either side of his box. This allowed the Tattenham Corner train to run under clear signals, straight into the back of the slow-moving Haywards Heath train. Some 31 passengers and the motorman of the Tattenham train lost their lives, and 183 passengers were hurt. Considering that over 514 passengers were standing in the two trains at the time of the collision, it is very fortunate that the signalman's error did not have even more serious consequences.

Photographs: Eltham Times Collection

BEATTOCK (BR-SCR)
8 June 1950

Fire has long been associated with railway disasters, but in reality, it is nearly always the result of an accident rather than an effect. There are a small number of incidents, however, where a fire has broken out in a moving train, Probably the worst example of such a disaster was near Westborough in 1941, when a coach was consumed by fire, claiming the lives of six schoolboys and injuring a number of others.

Some nine years later, on 8 June 1950, whilst the 11am Birmingham - Glasgow Central express made its way towards the summit at Beattock, a fire broke out on board the eleven-coach train. It appears to have started in the second coach, No. 4851, a three year-old Corridor Composite Third built for the LMS at Wolverton. The cause was attributed to a carelessly discarded match or cigarette-end being dropped in the sixth compartment shortly before the train arrived in Carlisle, and then rolled into or under the seat. The doors of the compartment were then closed, and because the fire was starved of oxygen, slow-combustion began. This helped intensely hot gases build-up inside the compartment, and though a few passengers thought they could smell smoke, it was put down as coming from the engine. Thus the fire went un-detected until an explosion blew out the corridor-side window of the compartment, and was followed by a fire-ball which swept through the coach, claiming the lives of five passengers. Just one person managed to escape from the coach, and this was only because they were in the toilet at the time of the explosion.

The train was brought to halt on Harthope Viaduct, and the actions of all the railwaymen are to be highly commended, particularly those of Ganger Adam Moffat. It was he who entered the blazing coach to rescue the solitary survivor, and then went back inside to see if he could help anyone else - for this heroic deed, he was later awarded the British Empire Medal. *Popperphoto Library*

FORD (BR-SR)
5 August 1951

On 5 August 1951, a serious accident in Sussex claimed the lives of eight passengers and a motorman, when an EMU over-ran danger signals and collided with another train which was being shunted due to insufficient platform space. Ford Station could easily accommodate the 4- and 6-coach EMU sets which normally worked the stopping trains, but in the height of summer 8-coach sets ran regularly at weekends and on some weekdays. At 11.52am a Three Bridges - Bognor train had arrived two minutes late at the station, where it was booked to wait five minutes to allow an 8-car Brighton - Portsmouth train to pass. This Sunday the Bognor train was also an 8-car affair, and thus too long for the loop platform so the signalman had to shunt it. However, as he had already accepted the other EMU into his section, he had to set his two home signals at danger. Though this would have delayed the Portsmouth train for a few minutes whilst the shunt was completed, it was a perfectly safe manoeuvre.

Regretfully the motorman of the incoming train over-ran both outer and inner home signals, and ploughed into the back of the Bognor train. This is one of the many cases where an accident happened because someone saw (or thought they saw) what they expected to see. In this instance the motorman of the Portsmouth train would have expected the Bognor train to be safely in the loop, and being under that impression he probably missed the signals as he drove his train into the station at about 25mph. As will be appreciated the 1937 stock, which made up both trains, did not stand up well to the impact. The trailing coach of the Bognor train and the leading coach of the Portsmouth train telescoped into each other, resulting in the fatalities and 47 serious injuries. Fortunately police, fire, and ambulance services were on the scene inside ten minutes, along with doctors and nurses. Valuable assistance was also rendered by personnel from the nearby Royal Naval Air Station, including a number of men with special rescue equipment.
Topham Picture Library

WATFORD (BR-LMR)
3 February 1954

On 3 February 1954, an accident occurred at Watford Junction Station which is of extreme interest because of its technical considerations more than the seriousness of the event - in fact no-one was killed or badly hurt and only 15 people suffered minor injuries or shock, though it could have been much worse. As the Up 'Royal Scot', 10.00am ex-Glasgow, headed by 8P class 4-6-0 No. 42650 *City of Lichfield* passed through Watford Tunnel, a rail broke when the 10-coach train passed over it. The trailing wheels of the ninth coach were derailed, and this was noticed by a passenger who pulled the communication cord. However, the train failed to stop, and the front of the engine only came to rest 1 mile 1,604 yards further on.

On reaching the point-work at Watford Junction Station, the rear part of the train broke free, and the trailing bogie of the eighth coach was pulled away. The ninth and tenth coach became completely derailed, and grazed the sides of the second to fifth coaches in the 4.37pm Euston - Wolverhampton which was passing through the station on the Down fast line. At first examination, it would seem that the permanent way staff had been negligent in allowing the track to deteriorate to a point where it was un-safe, and then that the driver and guard were at fault for allowing the train to run on for almost two miles after the initial derailment. Yet, the 25-page report into this accident did not reach that conclusion, although it did make a few minor observations in those directions. It would appear that the rail failure was due to a combination of design problems, both in locomotives and the permanent way. While in simulated tests after the accident, it was discovered how difficult it was to notice the 'gradual' brake application of the communication cord on a falling gradient.

This accident is one which we intend to cover in detail in *Back-Track,* for it is one which raises a host of technical considerations. Many readers of the magazine and *Trains In Trouble* have asked for more information on such matters, and it is our intention to provide the sort of information you want. However, if we are to come up with detailed articles on technical matters, such as Watford, we do need your help in tracing suitable pictures to illustrate them - so over to you! *Atlantic Collection*

CHAPEL-EN-LE-FRITH (BR-LMR)

9 February 1957

In a very few cases, a small number of accidents tragically occur due to a one-in-a-million chance when something completely unforeseen goes wrong. Such an event occurred at Chapel-en-le-Frith, Derbyshire, on 9 February 1957, when a class 8F goods locomotive got out of control and ran into the back of a preceding train. Working a Buxton - Arpley (Warrington) train, No. 48188, was handling an un-fitted freight comprised of 24 loaded coal wagons, 5 wagons of freight, 2 empty tank wagons, 2 loaded flat wagons, and a 20-ton brake van. As far as Bibbington's Sidings, the train was being banked by another class 8F, but on board the footplate of the train engine Driver John Axon and his fireman R. Scanlon were having problems with steam escaping from the driver's steam brake handle. This brake had leaked on their journey to Buxton, but it had been attended to by a fitter who tightened up the nut on the pipe which had apparently cured the problem. Now all they hoped for, was to get into the sidings where they could get assistance, then came a deafening bang and an explosion of escaping steam. This drove both men back to the tender, and though they tried to get to the controls they could neither make a full brake application or sound the whistle. The banker was still pushing hard at the rear, so Axon told Scanlon to jump off and drop as many wagon brakes as he could, whilst he tried to get to the control.

Scanlon managed to drop a few brakes, but the train was going too fast and it sped away down the incline. On arriving at Dove Holes loop, the signalman was faced with the un-enviable choice of either letting the engine crash there (and probably demolish his box in the process), or letting it run on in the hope that the driver could regain control. He chose the latter option, and then telephoned Chapel-en-le-Frith Central Station to inform them of the run-away, staff there acted with all promptitude and evacuated passengers from a 2-car DMU waiting in the Up platform. Regretfully, the preceding Down freight train, working from Rowsley to Stockport was just passing through the station, and there was little they could do to help them escape from Axon's train which was fast overhauling them. The 8F smashed into the back of the Rowsley train, killing the goods guard and demolishing a number of wagons, whilst the vehicles in the Buxton train piled up in a 25ft high heap behind No. 48188. Despite the opportunity to jump out of his cab, Axon displayed great courage and stayed with his train even though he must have been well aware of the danger. The accident was later attributed to a faulty braised collar on the steam brake pipe union, which had finally collapsed after it had been tightened at Buxton. The courage of the driver was recognized by the posthumous award of the George Cross, and later by the naming of a BR electric class 86, No. 86261, *Driver J. Axon GC.*

Photographs Courtesy: R. Leech Collection

PAISLEY (BR-ScR)
20 May 1958

Our collection of Scottish accidents continues with a collision at Arkleston Junction, near Paisley, on 20 May 1958, in which 97 people were injured when an engine and brake van hit a heavily loaded passenger train. As the 8-coach 7.15am train from Gourock to Glasgow headed towards the city, packed with commuters it proceeded through Arkleston Junction where an 0-6-0 tender engine was waiting to cross the four running lines with a 20-ton brake van. The driver of the 'J' class engine was a young, passed-fireman and his mate was a passed-cleaner, and both were quite inexperienced. Due to an error of judgement the driver took his engine across the path of the 2-6-4T on the passenger train, and the two collided at a combined speed of about 35mph.

The movement of the engine and van was, in many ways, a very complicated one, perhaps a little like a pedestrian trying to cross a busy road in the rush hour, and it required the driver to observe both fixed and hand signals. Such movements were frequently assigned to very inexperienced drivers, who in turn were only assisted by passed-cleaners and junior guards. Such work often being assigned as a prelude to yard shunting duties, but it is almost akin to letting a learner driver on to the M25 on a Monday morning. A moment's lapse in concentration, a mis-understood signal, or just lack of attention could lead to disaster - and at Paisley it did! The newspapers were quite critical about a system which placed so much responsibility on a novice driver, and in the official report Colonel Reed commented: 'It is all the more necessary, therefore, that the dual responsibilities of enginemen and guards on these occasions for observing signals should be brought home to junior men, both during teaching and examination, and during footplate supervision. It may be advisable to give more weight to this aspect of instruction for firemen and guards, and I would also suggest that some emphasis might be laid by supervisory staff..' Of those taken to hospital one person died of their injuries, and 26 others were detained. *Atlantic Collection*

LOCKWOOD (BR-NER)
28 June 1958

Lockwood Station on the Huddersfield - Penistone line was the scene of numerous accidents, nearly all of which were run-aways and one of these was featured in Volume 6. On 28 June 1958 another spectacular run-away occurred at the station, which actually started this writer's interest in railway accidents.

At 2.20pm signalman Firth at Lockwood No 2. box, situated at the junction of the line to Meltham, thought he could hear a train coming down the branch, but nothing was due. However, when he looked a rake of four empty coaches were running-away from a nearby siding on the branch. He quickly informed the signalmen at No.1 Box and Berry Brow, by sending the 4-5-5 (train running away) bell signal. The signalman at No. 1 box set the road for the coaches to pass through the Down goods yard, and into a very short spur which ended just above Swan Lane. However, the front portion of the rake smashed through the stop block, and leapt over the edge of an embankment. Flying above the road, the lead coach became embedded in the upper-part of the street-level booking office. Fortunately, the Station-master and booking clerk crawled out of the wrecked building without a scratch. Quite how this accident occurred is uncertain, but vandalism was suspected for it had become something of a local 'prank' for children to release wagon brakes.

The upper picture shows: The lift of lead coach M52504M beginning, but the detached leading bogie, now freed from captivity beneath the under-frame threatens to crash down the embankment into Swan Lane. In the end it was decided to let this happen, but in a controlled way - using hawsers to direct its fall.

The lower picture shows: Wakefield and Leeds (Holbeck MPD) breakdown cranes releasing the coach from the booking office, and preparing to lift it back to rail level before drawing it back over the coal drops siding. Photographs: P. Sunderland

BOROUGH MARKET (BR-SR)
12 August 1958

The problem of worn track is one which we have encountered before in this series, as for example in the accident at Grendon in Volume 5. That disaster has a great similarity to this featured accident which occurred at Borough Market in 1958. In both instances, the Permanent-way Inspector mis-calculated the life span of the track involved and, as a result of excessive wear a train was subsequently derailed.

The track-work in question was at the junction where the line from London Bridge Station diverges for Cannon Street and Charing Cross. As might be appreciated, this is an extremely busy junction, and the points that caused the derailment had no less than 275 booked train movements every weekday, resulting in exceptionally heavy wear. In such locations it was desirable to install longer-lasting manganese steel switch rails, but difficulties in supplies had meant that when the switches were replaced on 16 March that year, ordinary 95lb bull head carbon steel had to be employed. Previously, such switches had lasted between 12 to 14 months compared with the 17 to 22 months for manganese steel. Yet, following the introduction of ten-coach (4-car + 4-car + 2-car) EMU sets, the wear became even more rapid and a set of manganese steel switches installed the previous June had lasted just 9 months.

It is easy to understand how this situation was misjudged, but the wear led to the toe of the points breaking away, and in effect turned them into a ramp. On 12 August the first seven vehicles in the 6.52am Up train from Sanderstead to Cannon Street managed to negotiate these points safely, but the eighth coach was deflected. The rear two-car set was completely derailed and bounced against the parapet of the viaduct. Power supply to the tracks was cut off inside a minute, and all the passengers emerged little the worse for their ordeal. Six people were taken to hospital, though none of them were detained.
Atlantic Collection

BASCHURCH (BR-WR)
13 February 1961

On the evening of 13 February 1961 an unfitted freight train, which was equivalent to the length of 46 wagons was being taken from Coton Hill to Saltney by an ex-GWR 28XX class. When it arrived at Baschurch, between Oswestry and Shrewsbury, it was to be shunted to allow a following Down express to pass. Whilst setting back into a siding off the Down line, the driver felt resistance to his train and he stopped it, even though it was still marginally foul of the main line. The resistance was caused by the guard screwing down his brake prematurely, as he did not know whether his train was too long for the siding - which would actually accommodate 58 4-wheeled wagons. Though the driver did not 'pop' his whistle to signify he was fully in the siding, the signalman assumed he was, and cleared his signals for the 6.37pm express from Wellington to Chester.

Seeing the signals change, the freight driver assumed there had been a change of plan because his train was too long for the refuge and he slowly began to draw forward. He was just crossing the points when the engine of the express, Hall class 4-6-0 No. 6949, caught the leading vehicle in the goods train - a bogie bolster wagon - and then struck the rear of the 2-8-0's tender. *Haberfield Hall* overturned on to the Up line, and a stores-van next to the engine mounted the Up platform - the next vehicle, a corridor brake second, was thrown partially on top of the van. Coals from the engine must have fallen out, and the stores-van (a converted coach of 1908 vintage) caught fire. Two storesmen were riding in the van, and rescuers were unable to release one of them before the fire completely consumed the wooden shell. The driver and fireman of No. 6949 were also killed in the collision, but only two of the 22 passengers on board the six-coach train were slightly injured. The cause of the accident was entirely due to the failure of the signalman to ensure that the freight train was in the siding, but the driver and guard of that train also ought to have been more diligent. Under such circumstances, even the GWR's highly-efficient signalling system was unable to prevent a human failure of this type. Continuous track-circuiting would have made such an error highly unlikely, as would the provision of a loop siding rather than a refuge - both of which were installed shortly after the event!

Pictures: Eltham Times Collection

WATERLOO (BR-SR)
11 April 1961

Exactly two months after Baschurch, Britain's rail network suffered another fatal collision, this time at the approach to Waterloo Station. As the evening rush hour progressed on 11 April, precedence was being given to departing trains over those ending their journey. Though delays only averaged about three minutes, it was felt acceptable and so when an 8-car multiple unit arrived from Effingham Junction, it too was given a red signal. However the EMU failed to stop at the Outer-home, and it ran through the point-work at about 25 mph. Reversing out of the station at the same time (under clear signals), was a modified West Country Class 4-6-2, No.34040 *Crewkerne.* It had brought in the 1.25pm train from Weymouth, and was now running 'light engine' back to the motive power depot at about 12mph. As it was being driven tender-first, the driver had a restricted view and only saw the EMU just before the collision.

Though the EMU was of all-steel construction, the driving position offered little protection when it was hit head-on with such a considerable force. The motorman was killed outright, but in the train itself there were few casualties - of the 100 people on board only 14 reported any form of injury, and none were serious. However, something potentially more dangerous took place after the accident. When the accident occurred at 5.26pm, the circuit-breakers at Queens Road Sub-station tripped, and power to the line was cut off. Yet, the Down train to Horsham had been brought to a stand at the advance starting signal and, accidentally bridging the current-gap, it was allowing current to pass from the platform roads onto the supposedly 'safe' section. This was not discovered for some time, and during the intervening period all the passengers had been safely de-trained.

Though no-one was injured by this omission, the methods which were adopted after this accident took place were completely contrary to the procedures laid down in Southern Region's manual 'Instructions Applicable to Electrified Lines', and apparently no-one even thought of ensuring the safety of those walking around the crash-site by using short-circuiting bars. Quite why the motorman, who had an excellent record, over-ran the signals remains a mystery, though it is assumed he was simply not sufficiently observant. Just five days later the problems continued, when disaster struck at Pitsea (see Volume three) after 'an experienced and properly equipped man' made an error which derailed a ten-coach train to Shoeburyness. *Atlantic Collection*

CRICKLEWOOD (BR-LMR)
30 June 1962

The vast majority of the 'logged' accidents were minor affairs, and many of these took place in goods yards, engine sheds and carriage sidings where, to say the least, the track-work was not of the highest order. Despite the fact that they were very busy locations, signalling in these yards was also very basic, and in the majority of cases trains were moved under the control of a shunter's hand-signal. In almost every instance the movements were carried out in perfect safety, but just every now and then something went wrong. In this instance the drivers of a type 2 diesel, D5386, and Rolls Royce DMU both took the same hand-signal as permission for their train to draw out of Cricklewood Carriage Sidings. Both met at the fouling-point of the two sidings and scraped together but, as the picture shows, they were not seriously damaged.

Photograph Courtesy: A. Swain

RHIWDERIN (BR-WR)
7 February 1964

Welsh railways have not figured largely in this series and many of the smaller lines, like the Brecon & Merthyr Tydfil Junction, have been virtually ignored. This is not because of a lack of interest, but due entirely to a lack of suitable photographs. Therefore it is pleasing to show this picture of a 30-ton Cowans, Sheldon steam breakdown crane, No.139, in trouble on the B&M west of Bassaleg Junction. Details of the accident are scant, but it would appear, that whilst trying to lift a derailed steel-mineral wagon, the embankment collapsed beneath the crane's propping girders. Thus denied its stability, the crane rolled over on its side and slid down into the field, crushing the wagon it was trying to recover. It lay in this position for some time while a decision was taken about its future, but on 27 February work began on recovering the crane.

Photograph: the late E. Mountford, Courtesy P. Tatlow

RAYNES PARK (BR-SR)
28 November 1967

For our next account, we once again turn to the busy Southern Region, and witness the unusual results of a derailment on the former London & South Western Railway line at Raynes Park. During the early-morning of 28 November 1967, the 03.40 newspaper train from Waterloo to Farnborough was derailed as it approached the station. The 18-van train was travelling at a modest speed when the five rear vehicles were partially derailed, however one of the vans then completely left the rails. As it was passing the station footbridge, the van caught its supporting pillars, causing major structural damage. *The four-wheeled guard's van was pitched round and turned over, completely demolishing the body - and as the upper picture reveals, this would surely have killed anyone who was inside. However, with the greatest fortune the guard was riding elsewhere in the train at the time of the derailment and thus had the narrowest of escapes.*

One of the first tasks for the breakdown team, was to attend to the footbridge to prevent it from collapsing, and this work was given immediate priority. *The second picture shows the work being undertaken, using two breakdown cranes. Temporary props are being erected beneath the bridge whilst a mass of wreckage is strewn around the site.*

Our final picture shows the recovery operations at Raynes Park, with a 30-ton crane lifting an ex-SR Utility Van. Three other vans were also derailed across the tracks, seriously disrupting all traffic on the busy lines passing through Raynes Park. This had a knock-on effect at Waterloo, where passengers for Surbiton and Esher were urged to travel via the Windsor line and change at Teddington. After broadcasting this appeal, the station announcer was heard to say 'It is no use going to Wimbledon, there are too many passengers there already!'

Photographs Courtesy: P. Tatlow

BOSTON (BR-ER)
1969

For those readers in the railway modelling fraternity, who have suffered the frustration of having one of their locomotives jump the track - which only ever seems to happen when they are displaying at an exhibition - I have included this view taken in 1969. Immingham MPD's answer to 'big fingers in the sky', Cowans Sheldon 36-ton steam breakdown crane DB966103, rerails a class 08 shunter at Boston West Street Junction. Details of the event are obscure, and being a minor derailment was not subject to an Accident Report. However, it does portray a relatively common type of incident where a locomotive got into trouble. Also typical is the attitude of the workmen in the scene, a small band work hard on the rerailing, the rest stand back with arms folded or with their hands in pockets - a little like our house when it comes to the gardening!
Photograph: N.H. Pigott, courtesy P. Tatlow Collection.

ABERDEEN (BR-ScR)
May 1970

Despite the apparently easy task witnessed at Boston, rerailing operations were not always simple, and sometimes they led to even further complications when a problem developed with the lifting equipment. Such an incident was noted on Aberdeen's Waterloo Branch, when the match-truck to a Cowans, Sheldon 30 ton steam break-down crane was derailed during a call-out. The rerailing should have been a fairly simple operation, but it would seem that the crane crew took its simplicity for granted and failed to pull out the propping girders. With the lack of stability the centre of gravity was seriously affected, and the former LMS crane toppled over on its side with the jib coming to rest on the wall of a nearby factory. According to a former Cowans, Sheldon design-engineer, 'a quick recovery job like this could probably have been undertaken 999 times without the propping girders being extended, and no ill-effect would have been seen - but the girders were there for the 1,000th.' Whatever, the fate of RS1074/30 just goes to reinforce his statement that 'nothing should ever be taken for granted'.
Photograph: J. Templeton courtesy P. Tatlow Collection.

GUILDFORD (BR-SR)
28 July 1971

On Wednesday 28 July 1971, four platforms at Guildford Station (No.s 5-8) were blocked when a parcel train headed by Birmingham RCW class 33 No. 6561 became derailed at 4.30 in the morning. The van behind the locomotive was also derailed, and the resulting blockage had a considerable effect on the morning's commuter traffic.

In order not to delay commuter trains to London and Woking, workings from Redhill to Reading were curtailed. Only two early trains, one to Ascot and one to Waterloo, were cancelled. It was later reported that, even at the busiest times Waterloo trains were only running ten minutes behind schedule. Rerailing operations, pictured here, began at 9.30am when the rush hour traffic had subsided and the Cowans Sheldon 75 ton crane DB9651-64 could get into position. Through running was established by just after lunch.
Surrey Advertiser Photograph.

GLOUCESTER (BR-WR)
7 May 1972

Whilst running 'light engine' to Cheltenham on 7 May 1972, a pair of Type 1 Bo-Bo Diesel-Electric locomotives (class 20s) from Saltley Depot ended up 'off all-wheels' on the outskirts of Gloucester. As these locomotives approached Barnwood Junction they over-ran the signals which were set at danger, and were derailed to the left of the track by a pair of catch-points. The leading locomotive ran down a slight embankment and came to rest at an angle of about 30 degrees, though D8155 bringing up the rear remained more or less in an upright position.

The rerailing operation is seen in progress, with two cranes commencing the lift of D8155. Of specific interest is the ex-GWR locomotive tender which forms part of the nearest breakdown train. This tender had been retained to act as a water bowser for the Ransome & Rapier steam breakdown crane, thus proving that even after August 1968 steam operations were still being regularly carried out on main line British railways.
Photograph Courtesy: T.W. Nichols

STOULTON (BR-WR)
30 November 1984

Though derailments like Sevenoaks and Watford can still occur, modern technology has done much to minimise the risk to passengers. This can clearly be seen from an accident at Stoulton, between Worcester and Pershore, on Wednesday 30 November when a track failure led to a major derailment. The train was the 7.05am Hereford to London express, which was just attaining 75pmh after its stop in Worcester. Due to a fish-plate fault the train derailed and ran along the ballast, distorting the single track line so badly that it looked like a narrow gauge railway. The back four coaches broke free and piled up round an over-line bridge, but the strength of the modern coaching stock prevented a repeat of Sevenoaks though, as the picture shows, the conditions were not dissimilar. Only two passengers were slightly hurt, and they were able to continue their journey after treatment in the local hospital.

Photo. by kind permission of Worcester Evening News, Berrows Newspapers Ltd.

CHINLEY (BR-LMR)
20 February 1987

Whilst working a limestone train down the branch from Peak Forest, No. 47089 *Amazon* got out of control and was derailed on trap points protecting the main line from Manchester to Sheffield. The class 47 turned on its side, and due to the momentum its train of 'Covhop' wagons piled up around the locomotive. Some of the debris spilled over on to the Down-main line, fouling the path of an approaching loco-hauled train from Sheffield. Regretfully, due to the sharply curved cutting on the approach to the North Junction, the driver of No.31440 only became aware of the obstruction at the very last moment. The class 31 struck the debris causing major damage to the near-side cab corner, but the driver had time to move from his seat and no injuries resulted. Our photograph was taken the following day, 21 February, and shows clearing-up operations being performed by 75 ton cranes from Doncaster and Toton (nearest camera). Following this accident the trap-points were re-positioned further back from the junction, and a sand-drag was installed at the end of it.

Photograph. M.S. Welch

COPYHOLD JUNC. (BR-SR)
14 June 1988

On 14 June 1988, No. 56062, whilst working an Ardingly (ARC Stone Terminal) - Westbury empty, failed to stop at the trap-points protecting the main London - Brighton line at Copyhold Junction just north of Haywards Heath. The trap fulfilled its task, but the engine was derailed along with a number of wagons and they rolled 20 feet down a steep embankment. Only the train guard sustained slight injuries. However, that wasn't the end of the potential danger, for the locomotive came to rest on the top of a large gas main. Fortunately the fire-services and gas board officials took steps to ensure that no explosion attended the accident.

Recovery from the base of the embankment would be difficult, and for some time BR engineers deliberated whether or not this would be its final resting place. However, it was decided against cutting it up on the spot, though a great deal of civil engineering had to be undertaken before any recovery operations could begin. The embankment was first stabilized, then sufficiently reinforced with piling and a concrete pad in order to take the weight of two recovery cranes in addition to that of the damaged locomotive once it was lifted. On 18 August the Railfreight loco. was raised into an upright position with the use of air bags and packing, but it was a full seventeen days before breakdown cranes from Eastleigh and Wimbledon depots were able to lift out the diesel engine and alternator unit. On 2 October the same cranes were back again, lifting the body shell off the bogies, which in turn were retrieved from the crash site. No. 56062 was taken to Doncaster Works, where it was rebuilt and subsequently put back into service. *Upper View: The badly damaged locomotive laying at the foot of the embankment - an unsure fate awaiting it. Lower View: Lifting out the engine from No. 56062 on 4 September 1988.*

Photographs Courtesy: Bryan Ridge

HUDDERSFIELD (BR-ER)
6 November 1989

As I closed my account in Volume 6 with news of an accident at Huddersfield which occurred on the night I was finalizing that volume, it is only fitting that I should conclude this present series of accounts with a view of the incident in question.

On 7 November 1989 a collision between two DMUs (a class 141 and a 'Sprinter') happened on the approach to Huddersfield Viaduct, quite close to the scene of the 1905 Huddersfield Viaduct Accident recounted in Volume 5. The trains involved in the more recent event were the 19.48 ex-Scarborough 'Sprinter' for Liverpool, and the 21.26 from Huddersfield to Wakefield Westgate. The Scarborough train was checked on its approach to Huddersfield, and brought to a stand by a signal 500 yards east of the station; the Wakefield train was leaving the station, and slowly picking up speed to somewhere between 15 and 20 mph. In all, some 55 passengers were aboard the two 2-car DMUs, and many were thrown from their seats sustaining minor injuries, cuts and bruising. Fire-appliances and a fleet of ambulances were quickly on the scene, and firemen carried passengers to the station. Seventeen passengers were taken to the local infirmary, but the only casualty detained was the guard of the Wakefield train.

The cause of the accident was later attributed to problems associated with the re-signalling work which was being carried out at the time. Huddersfield's colour-light signalling system dated back to 1958, which had replaced two manual boxes with a single control room on the island platform. On Sunday 5 November, BR engineers had been replacing these signals as part of a new £2-million improvement scheme. Hand signalling had been instituted on the previous day, and it was still in operation when the accident occurred. The class 150 'Sprinter' came out of the accident with only minor damage to the corridor connection and the cable junction boxes, but the main-frame of 141-104 was badly distorted and, though our picture appears to show only superficial damage, the car was subsequently scrapped. Ironically, this accident took place on the eve of the publication of the report on the Clapham disaster, which (in part) recommended a revision of signalling practices on BR.
Huddersfield Examiner Photographs

WHEEL MEET AGAIN

As we come to the end of Volume seven, this reflective photograph shows the last days of No. 32327, a former LB&SCR 4-6-4T which had been rebuilt into a 'Remembrance Class 4-6-0. The engine had been working a Waterloo - Basingstoke train on 23 December 1955, and at Woking had overhauled and run into the rear of a Portsmouth train which had left Waterloo 4 minutes earlier. The damage was too great for economic repair, and she was withdrawn at Eastleigh works the following month. With the front end stoved in, twisted frames and missing bogie, she has been stripped of her final dignity with the removal of the coupling rods and name plate.

We too have reached the end of our present offering, but a good deal of material has been amassed for future publication. In our final book we hope to conclude the story by incorporating even more historic accidents along with a comprehensive index to the series. Of course we still have much to find, with notable omissions such as Elliot Junction, St. Bede's Junction, Little Salkeld (1918), Castlecary, Lichfield, Weedon (1951) and Sutton Coldfield thus-far eluding our extensive research. Our previous appeals to you have generated an exceptionally pleasing response, so we hope to hear from you again with details of accident and incident photographs. So, perhaps it is fitting to use this photograph of No. 32327, *Trevithick,* in inviting would be contributors to contact Atlantic at Trevithick House. *Photograph Courtesy: S.C. Townroe*